PRIMARY SOURCES OF THE THIRTEEN COLONIES AND THE LOST COLONY ™

A Primary Source History of the Colony of

NEW JERSEY

TAMRA ORR

rosen central
Primary Source™

The Rosen Publishing Group, Inc., New York

Published in 2006 by The Rosen Publishing Group, Inc.
29 East 21st Street, New York, NY 10010

First Edition

Library of Congress Cataloging-in-Publication Data

Orr, Tamra.
A primary source history of the colony of New Jersey/by Tamra Orr.
    p. cm.—(Primary sources of the thirteen colonies and the Lost Colony)
ISBN 1-4042-0430-X (lib. bdg.)
ISBN 1-4042-0668-X (pbk. bdg.)

1. New Jersey—History—Colonial period, ca. 1600–1775—Juvenile literature. 2. New Jersey—History—1775–1865—Juvenile literature.
I. Title. II. Series.

F137.O77 2006
974.9'01—dc22

2004023491

Manufactured in the United States of America

On the front cover: An oil painting by Howard Pyle entitled *The Landing of Carteret in New Jersey*.

CONTENTS

INTRODUCTION

Change and Continuity

It is always difficult to look at a densely populated, highly developed, and bustling state and imagine it as it was long ago, before people, roads, and buildings came along and changed the landscape entirely. This is certainly true for New Jersey and its skyscrapers, highways, refineries, corporate parks, shopping malls, and eight and a half million residents.

Yet, throughout its colonial history, New Jersey was a densely forested rural territory celebrated for its abundant natural resources and rich farmland. Characterized by religious tolerance and a live-and-let-live attitude, New Jersey became a haven for people who desired only to work hard and build a peaceful and prosperous life for themselves and their families. Though the landscape of New Jersey has changed drastically, in many ways its founding spirit has not.

This spirit of diversity, tolerance, industriousness, and individual liberty was what made New Jersey such a prosperous and relatively peaceful colony, and such an important player in the American Revolution. The legacy of the colony's founding spirit is still in evidence in New Jersey, the third state admitted into the Union. Indeed, to this day, New Jersey remains one of the most diverse, productive, and flourishing states in the country. Though the Lenape and early colonists—who lived and worked in heavily forested tracts and rolling, open farmland—would recognize little of the modern Garden State's landscape, they would certainly be familiar with the energy and optimism of New Jersey residents and the rich opportunities open to them.

The dramatic extent of New Jersey's growth, development, and change is graphically illustrated by these two views of the Passaic River. Both views depict nearly the same location on the river, just below the Passaic Falls, though they are separated by about 200 years. The photograph *(top)* was taken in the late twentieth century while the painting *(bottom)*, by Alexander Robertson, was made in 1798.

CHAPTER 1

As hard as it may be to picture today, the land that would one day be New Jersey was once the heavily wooded home of a tribe called the Lenni Lenape, which means "original people." They spoke a dialect of the Algonquian language and were referred to by Europeans as the Delaware, because they had settled the Delaware River area (including present-day Delaware, eastern Pennsylvania, New Jersey, and southeastern New York). Some historians believe they occupied this area of the world for as many as 10,000 years. Some Lenape oral traditions suggest that this region was the birthplace of all the Algonquin tribes.

The Lenape and the Arrival of the Europeans

The Lenape relied heavily on hunting and planting for survival. They farmed everything from beans to squash and corn, and they harvested the wild blueberries, strawberries, and cranberries that grew in the area. The region was rich with wildlife, including deer, foxes, squirrels, raccoons, mink, and bears. There were even wild geese and turkeys living in the forests, and the Lenape often wore their feathers as decoration.

In the spring, the Lenape would travel from the interior of the region to the seashore for several months, much like today's residents of New Jersey. The footpaths they made to and from the shore would one day become the wagon roads settlers would follow to crisscross the colony. The Lenape spent each day at the sea fishing for clams, oysters, other shellfish, and other types of

A Lenape couple is depicted in this circa 1640 drawing by Swedish cartographer and engineer Peter Lindestrom. Originally, the name Lenape may have referred only to Native Americans living along a portion of the west bank of the Delaware River. Only later would it come to be used to refer to the entire Algonquian-speaking population of the Mid-Atlantic coast. Traders from Sweden and the Netherlands were the first Europeans to occupy the lands of the Lenape. Though the first explorer to the area, Giovanni da Verrazano, found the Lenape to be sweet and gentle, Lindestrom considered them to be mischievous and deceitful.

edible sea life. The day's catch would either provide that night's meal or be smoked and dried for use during the lean winter months. The Lenape would travel across the ocean and area rivers in canoes they had made by burning and scraping out the center of huge, heavy logs.

Most of the Lenape lived in homes called wigwams, which were roundhouses made from tree saplings that were pushed into the ground and then tied together. The outsides of the buildings were covered with tree bark and grass. A hole was always left in the wigwam's roof for ventilation and to let the smoke of wood fires escape out of the dwelling. Some tribes also

Some modern New Jersey cities still carry Lenape names. Here is what they mean:

Allamuchy	place within the hills
Alloway	more
Cheesequake	land that has been cleared
Cinnaminson	rocky place of fish
Hackensack	mouth of a river
Hoboken	tobacco pipe
Kittatinny	big mountain
Manahawkin	where the land slopes
Manasquan	place to gather grass
Neshanic	two creeks
Passaic	valley
Watchung	hilly place

built longhouses, which were rectangular buildings covered in bark. These could house many people and were preferred by those Lenape with larger families.

The "Discovery" of New Jersey

The first European to "discover" New Jersey was an Italian explorer named Giovanni da Verrazano. In 1524, he crossed the ocean in a ship called *La Dauphine* on the orders of Francis I, the king of France. The king wanted him to explore the unknown area between Florida and Newfoundland, Canada. He was curious to learn if a direct sea route to the Pacific Ocean existed. Verrazano's voyage was backed financially by wealthy Italian merchants and bankers living in France who would have much to gain by the discovery of a direct route to the Asian lands that were fabled for their wealth.

On July 8, 1524, while still on board the ship *La Dauphine*, the explorer, Giovanni da Verrazano *(above right)*, wrote to his patron, King Francis I, to describe his voyage to the New World. In his report, Verrazano describes the stormy crossing of the Atlantic Ocean, his first landing on the shore of what would become New Jersey, his first contact with the Lenape, and his discovery of what would later be named New York Harbor, Manhattan, the Hudson River, and Block Island and Newport, Rhode Island. Verrazano also reports his conclusion that the land he has discovered is part of a huge continent that forms an obstacle between Europe and his original goal—Asia—indicating that Earth is far larger than previously believed. See the transcript on page 55.

The explorer dropped his anchor north of present-day Sandy Hook but only remained a short time. While *La Dauphine* remained anchored out at sea, Verrazano sent a boat to shore to meet with the Lenape who had assembled there. Some of them even came on board the ship. Verrazano wrote, "They came without fear aboard our ship. This is the goodliest people and of the fairest conditions that we have found in this our voyage," as quoted in R. Conrad Stein's *New Jersey*.

Verrazano sent a full report back to King Francis I, detailing what he could of the land and of the people he had encountered. When he landed, there were anywhere from 8,000 to 10,000 Lenape living in the area. We have a record of Verrazano's first impressions, but what must the Lenape have thought when they first laid eyes on that strange wooden sea creature filled with white people who spoke a strange and incomprehensible language and dressed in outlandish clothing?

The Discovery Continues

Verrazano's visit was so brief, it had little impact on the Lenape and their way of life. That all changed, however, with the arrival of English explorer Henry Hudson on board the *Half Moon* in 1609. Because he could not persuade anyone in England to give him the financial backing he needed, Hudson had sailed across the Atlantic Ocean on behalf of the Dutch. Like Verrazano, he was searching for what was called the Northwest Passage, which was thought to cut right through North America and lead directly to Asia. Several European nations wanted to find a quick and reliable water route to Asia, as it was rumored to be a land of unlimited riches and treasures, such as gold, jewels, and spices.

Like Verrazano almost a century before him, Hudson dropped anchor near Sandy Hook. He and his men were uncomfortable around the Lenape, however. They did not trust them, despite the generous kindness with which the Lenape greeted the strangers. A crew member named Robert Juet wrote in his journal, "This day the people of the Countrey came

GIOVANNI DA VERRAZANO'S REPORT TO FRANCIS I, JULY 8, 1524: THE HISTORY OF *LA DAUPHINE* AND ITS VOYAGE

Upon his return to France, the explorer Giovanni da Verrazano provided King Francis I with a full written report of his voyage to the New World. This is what he wrote in his report about his encounter with and impressions of the Lenni Lenape and the land around present-day Sandy Hook:

After a hundred leagues we found a very agreeable place between two small but prominent hills; between them a very wide river, deep at its mouth, flow out into the sea; and with the help of the tide, which rises eight feet, any laden ship could have passed from the sea into the river estuary [Sandy Hook and New York Harbor]. Once we were anchored off the coast and well sheltered, we did not want to run any risks without knowing anything about the river mouth. So we took the small boat up this river to land which we found densely populated. The people were almost the same as the others, dressed in birds' feathers of various color and they came toward us joyfully, uttering loud cries of wonderment, and showing us safest place to beach the boat. We went up this river for about half a league [1.5 miles (2.4 km)], where we saw that it formed a beautiful lake, about three leagues [9 miles (14.5 km)] in circumference. About 30 small boats ran to and from across the lake with innumerable people aboard who were crossing from one side to the other to see us. Suddenly, as often happens in sailing, a violent unfavorable wind blew in from the sea, and we were forced to return to the ship, leaving the land with much regret on account of its favorable conditions and beauty; we think [it] was not without some properties of value, since all the hills showed signs of minerals.

—As quoted in *The Voyages of Giovanni da Verrazano*, edited by Lawrence C. Wroth

aboard to us, seeming very glad of our comming," as quoted in Wendy Moragne's *New Jersey*. Later on, according to Steve Wick's article "*Half Moon* Arriving," Juet added,

> Our men went on Land there, and saw great store of Men, Women and Children, who gave them Tabacco at their coming on Land. So they went up into the Woods, and saw great store of goodly Oakes and some Currants. For one of them came aboord and brought some dryed, and gave me some, which were sweet and good. This day many of the people came aboord, some in Mantles of Feathers, and some in Skinnes of divers sorts of good Furres. Some women also came to us with Hempe. They had red Copper Tabacco pipes, and other things of Copper they did weare about their neckes. At night they went on Land againe, so wee rode very quiet, but durst not trust them.

Perhaps because of this distrust, things did not go well between Hudson's men and the Lenape. When Hudson sent five of his men out to explore another river a dozen miles to the north, they were attacked by Lenape in canoes. The leader of this small party, John Coleman, was killed by an arrow to his throat, and two of his men were seriously injured. The *Half Moon* remained anchored all night and kept a close watch for any further trouble.

The next day, the Lenape came on board the ship to trade with the Europeans. Juet wrote that everyone kept an eye out to "see if they would show any sign of the death of our man, which they did not. In an attempt to deceive us, [they] pretended interest in buying knives. But we were aware of their intent and took two of them prisoners." The men planned to hold the Lenape as

Henry Hudson's first encounter with the Lenape in 1609 is depicted in this oil painting *(top)*. In the background can be seen his ship, the *Half Moon*, anchored off what would become Sandy Hook, New Jersey. His explorations along the modern-day New Jersey and New York coasts and up the river that now bears his name would make possible later Dutch settlement of the area. In 1614, the New Netherland Company was formed to engage in fur trading in the area. In 1623, the Dutch West India Company had the area recognized as a Dutch province, named New Netherland, and settlement and trading began to flourish. This circa 1648 map *(right)* of New Netherland was made by Adriaen van der Donck, a gentleman landowner and saw mill operator who lived north of Manhattan.

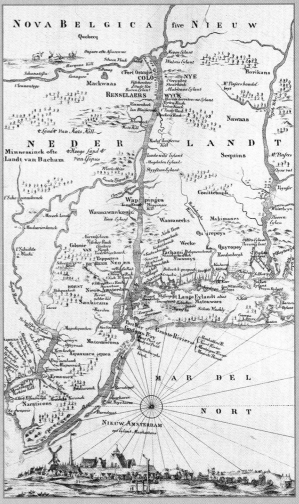

13

hostages to help prevent another attack. Hudson wrote that he was prepared to order his men to kill the Lenape hostages if they betrayed any signs of guilt for the murder. Two more Lenape were taken as prisoners, but all the hostages either jumped overboard and escaped or were released. Hudson set sail the next day, but not before claiming the land for his employers, the Dutch.

Five years later, in 1614, Dutch captain Cornelius Mey sailed into the mouth of the Delaware River. He stayed long enough to build a tiny fort near the present-day town of Gloucester. Cape May, at the southern tip of the state, is named for him. Almost two decades would pass before Europeans would return to Lenape territory, this time as settlers.

Despite the tension Hudson had created with the Lenape, the explorer had also opened the way for settlers and traders to journey to this new region. The Lenape were about to be confronted with a harsh new reality—it was time to share the land that they had inhabited for thousands of years. New faces were on the horizon.

CHAPTER 2

The Dutch and the English

Henry Hudson's discovery and claim of the area now being called New Netherland (encompassing present-day New York, New Jersey, and part of Connecticut) inspired many Dutch settlers to move there. Large numbers of Swedes and Finns soon followed them by the late 1630s. Many were lured there by the stories they heard about the richness of the land.

In the beginning, the Swedish and Dutch settlers got along quite well with each other as well as with the Lenape. As in many instances throughout early American history, the Native Americans taught the settlers a great deal about how to survive on this new, rugged, and often harsh land. They showed them how to hunt, fish, and trap in the region's forests and rivers. They taught them about the area's seasonal cycles and the best plants to grow, given the weather, climate, and soil type. The Lenape even traded some land in return for clothes, guns, knives, and ritual beads. In return, the Swedes taught them how to construct log cabins similar to those in which they had lived in Sweden. The ones the Swedes and Lenape built were the first log cabins ever constructed in the United States.

Both the Dutch and the Swedes began trading for animal furs with the Lenape. Fur was all the rage throughout Europe, and pelts were in high demand. For little cost to the settlers, they could obtain furs from the Lenape and turn around and sell them in Europe for a large profit. While this was an enterprising idea, it also began causing conflict and competition between the two

Trading activity between Swedish settlers and the Delaware, or Lenape, is depicted in this seventeenth-century sketch *(top)*. In 1637, Swedish, Dutch, and German stockholders formed the New Sweden Company to trade for furs and tobacco in North America. In 1638, the settlers began to build a fort—named Fort Christina—at the site of present-day Wilmington, Delaware. It was the first permanent European settlement in the Delaware River valley. The colony grew and eventually consisted of farms and small settlements along both banks of the Delaware River into present-day Delaware, New Jersey, Pennsylvania, and Maryland. One of the main articles of trade between the Lenape and the Swedes were beaver pelts, like the one seen here *(bottom)*, stretched on a wooden frame as part of the tanning (or softening) process.

groups of settlers. The Swedes were particularly harsh with the Lenape and adopted a "be assimilated or be annihilated" attitude toward them. Because the Dutch were kinder to them, the Lenape formed alliances with them in order to protect their way of life. By 1655, the Dutch, led by Peter Stuyvesant, director general of New Netherland, had forced most of the Swedes out of the region. This proved to be just a temporary improvement for the Lenape. With the Swedes vanquished, the Dutch began to argue with the Lenape over land and fur. Soon, violence between the former friends broke out, and there were deaths on both sides.

Meanwhile, small trading villages were springing up in the present-day areas of Hoboken and Jersey City. In 1660, the town of Bergen was established by the Dutch, becoming New Jersey's first permanent settlement and its first local civil government. Bergen and surrounding villages grew over the years and eventually were incorporated into present-day Jersey City.

England Takes Control

In 1664, the entire region of New Netherland was conquered by England and claimed for James, the Duke of York. In turn, James, who would eventually become King James II, gave a large part of the territory between the Hudson and Delaware Rivers to two of his most loyal supporters, Lord John Berkeley and Sir George Carteret. In honor of Jersey, an island in the English Channel that he had governed, Carteret dubbed the land New Jersey.

Berkeley and Carteret were not only loyal subjects to the Crown, but they were also enterprising young men with a flair for business. They saw an opportunity to profit from this new land. They wanted to charge rental fees on each plot of land carved out of the territory.

A MARKETING CAMPAIGN

New Jersey settlers were encouraged by colonial authorities to write to friends and family back in England and urge them to move to the colony by praising (and often exaggerating) the land's bounty and the unlimited possibilities and freedoms of the New World. Because the colony's primary purpose was to generate income for the mother country, colonial authorities wanted to attract as many settlers as possible and to encourage development and economic activity. This is an example of a promotional letter written in 1676:

Dear and loving friend John Sunison,

My kind love unto thee and to thy wife, hoping these lines may find thee in good health, as thanks be unto the Lord, we are all safe through mercy arrived at New Caesarea or New Jersey . . .

    If any are minded to come over, they may go thither and know what goods to bring that are fit to sell or use here. Here is not want of anything but good people to inhabit. Here is liberty for the honest-hearted that truly desire to fear the Lord. Here is liberty from the cares and bondage of this world, and after one year or two, you may live very well with very little labor. Here is great store of fish and fowl, and plenty of corn, and cows, hogs, horses, oxen, sheep, venison, nuts, strawberries, grapes, and peaches. Here is good English wheat, ripe in three months. Wheat is 4 shillings a bushel, barley at three, good white rye at three, good Indian corn at 2 shillings, 6 pence a bushel. Half a bushel when it is planted will find a great family a whole year with bread and drink … The beef fats itself, and hogs fat themselves. They are fat all the year, and people may kill them when they have occasion. Here is good land enough, and wood enough. Servants are in great request. Young men and maids come to great fortune . . . and do very well . . .

My mother remembers her to thee, and she would not have you be discouraged, because of the water, for the Lord is well able to preserve by sea and land. We were near two hundred people on board the ship we came in. There was an ancient woman judged near four score of age, and she did very well. And several others that were very ancient. We lost but two . . . I rest, thy loving friend till death,

Esther Huckens
Delaware, New Jersey
April the 4th, 1676

—Text of letter provided by the New Jersey
Historical Commission

In order to do that, they needed to create demand for these plots by persuading English citizens to move to New Jersey.

To attract settlers, they offered several different enticements or "concessions." They offered farms to anyone "having a good musket and six months' provisions" free of charge for the first five years. Rent on the land would be deferred (put off) until 1670, and when it began, it would be set low—a half-penny an acre. There would be no taxation without representation, meaning the interests of New Jersey settlers would be represented by a government that included a governor, a council, and an assembly of twelve representatives chosen by the people. Best of all, Carteret and Berkeley promised total political and religious toleration. In other words, no political viewpoints or faiths would be outlawed,

Sir George Carteret was born on the English island of Jersey, where his family had been prominent landowners for many generations. As a Royalist during the English Civil War, Carteret supported Prince Charles in his attempts to subdue Parliament and reinstate the monarchy. In return for his support, Charles granted Carteret a small group of islands near Virginia, which were to be called New Jersey. Carteret was forced to surrender this land, however, when Prince Charles was defeated by the parliamentary forces. After the restoration of the monarchy, James, the Duke of York, the future King James II, rewarded Carteret for his long, loyal service on behalf of the royal Stuart family by granting his New World holdings between the Delaware and Hudson rivers to Carteret and another supporter, John Berkeley. In honor of his birthplace, Carteret named the the territory New Jersey.

unlike in England. That was a huge attraction for those who had suffered for their beliefs; many people left England for the colonies in order to escape religious and political persecution. One of the persecuted religious groups to whom Carteret and Berkeley rented land was the Religious Society of Friends, better known as the Quakers.

The Religious Society of Friends

The Religious Society of Friends is a Christian sect that got its start around 1648. Its nickname refers to the physical quaking that some worshippers felt during an intense religious experience. The basic philosophy of the religion was taught by a man named George Fox. The mainstream Christian churches he had attended had all left him dissatisfied. He was looking for a more immediate religious experience, a more direct communication with God. His ideas about how to achieve this were quite blasphemous at the time.

Fox firmly believed that all people could have a direct, personal, one-on-one relationship with God. He felt that people did not need to speak with clergymen (ministers, priests, pastors, etc.) to help them communicate with God. As Fox put it, "Why should any man have power over any other man's faith, seeing Christ himself is the author of it?" He also taught that the Bible was not the word of God—the utterances of God given directly to humans—but a book written by a variety of men living at various times and working under the influence of the Holy Spirit. Fox encouraged all people who joined his religious society to simply be silent and listen for God during church services. In this silence, God might speak directly to them and, in doing so, impart special powers.

Puritans

At the same time Berkeley and Carteret were handing out parcels of land to the Quakers, the governor of New York, Richard Nicolls, was handing out the same parcels of land to a religious group called the Puritans, under a grant called the Monmouth Patent. Nicolls was not aware that the Duke of York had given New Jersey to Berkeley and Carteret. The Puritans and the Quakers were both members of dissenting religions, meaning they stood in opposition to the Church of England, the dominant, state-supported Christian church in England. Yet, despite their shared dissent, the beliefs of the Puritans and the Quakers were extremely different from each other. Quakers were pacifists and were devoted to the dignity and equality of every human being. They felt every individual could have a direct and personal relationship with God, without the help of ritual, ministers, or even doctrine and teaching. The Puritans, on the other hand, insisted upon strict obedience to Bible teachings and God's law, hard work, and harsh punishment for sins.

Settlers Arrive

Although Berkeley and Carteret were the proprietors of this new land, they never actually came to New Jersey in person. Instead, they sent Carteret's fourth cousin, Philip Carteret, to govern in their place. He and thirty others arrived in New Jersey in 1665 and founded the settlement of Elizabethtown (named in honor of Sir George Carteret's wife).

The settlers began to arrive soon after, thanks to Carteret and Berkeley's heavy marketing campaign in England. In addition, a large number of Puritans began arriving from New England. The area's earlier Dutch, Swedish, and Finnish settlers, their slaves, and

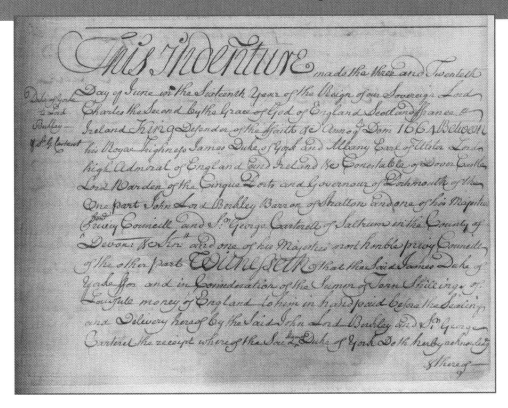

On June 16, 1664, James, the Duke of York, signed an indenture (a formal document) granting the territory that would become New Jersey to his loyal followers George Carteret and John Berkeley. In the document, James describes the extent and boundaries of the territory as follows: "[A]ll that tract of land adjacent to New England, and lying and being to the westward of Long Island, and Manhitas Island [Manhattan] and bounded on the east part by the main sea [the Atlantic Ocean], and part by Hudson's river, and hath upon the west Delaware bay or river, and extendeth southward to the main ocean as far as Cape May at the mouth of the Delaware bay; and to the northward as far as the northermost branch of the said bay or river of Delaware, which is forty-one degrees and forty minutes of latitude, and crosseth over thence in a strait line to Hudson's river in forty-one degrees of latitude; which said tract of land is hereafter to be called by the name or names of New Caeserea or New Jersey." See the transcript on pages 55–56.

the Lenape were now joined by English, Scottish, Irish, and Scots-Irish colonists (the Scots-Irish were Scots who had earlier immigrated to the north of Ireland beginning in the early seventeenth century). New Jersey was now one of the most ethnically

Quakers in seventeenth-century England were subjected to oppression and ridicule not only by the government but also by other influential segments of society. This seventeenth-century painting of a Quaker meeting criticizes the worshippers by depicting them in a physically unflattering light. The artist, Egbert van Heemskerk, was a passionate anti-Quaker who was especially offended by the Quakers' mingling of the sexes during worship services and by women's right to speak at meetings (as is pictured here). Van Heemskerk was a Dutch painter working mostly in London who specialized in tavern scenes and peasant celebrations.

diverse colonies in the British Empire. To this day, it remains one of the most diverse states in the Union.

Many of the newly arrived families made their living by farming, while others set up small businesses. Tanneries were opened to turn cowhides into leather goods. Sawmills took felled trees and turned them into lumber for construction. Gristmills ground harvested wheat and turned it into flour for baking.

CHAPTER 3

P hilip Carteret's job as the first governor of New Jersey was not an easy one. Conflicts were breaking out between the settlers and the Lenape, as well as between the Quakers and the Puritans. Which of these groups really owned the land? When were rents due? How much would they be? To whom were they paid? These questions were about to become even more complicated as New Jersey began to pull apart at the seams. Indeed, the colony would soon be literally divided in half.

A Colony Torn in Two

A Territory Divided

Big changes were in store for the newly named New Jersey. When the rent deferment offered by John Berkeley and George Carteret ended in 1670, and Philip Carteret attempted to gather the settlers' land payments, he was met with anger and resistance. The Puritans claimed that they had gotten their land under Governor Nicoll's Monmouth Patent, so they felt no obligation to pay anything to Carteret. Other settlers claimed to have received their land from the Lenape, who had a far older claim to the territory than either Governor Carteret or Governor Nicolls.

These settlers had become accustomed to frontier-style self-government and wanted to preserve this New World liberty. Carteret collected little rent money, and, at the same time, people began to dislike him and resent the English claims of ownership of the land. Finally, the Duke of York stepped in and declared that any land titles given under the Monmouth Patent were illegal. The Puritans were so angry with this decision that they held an illegal

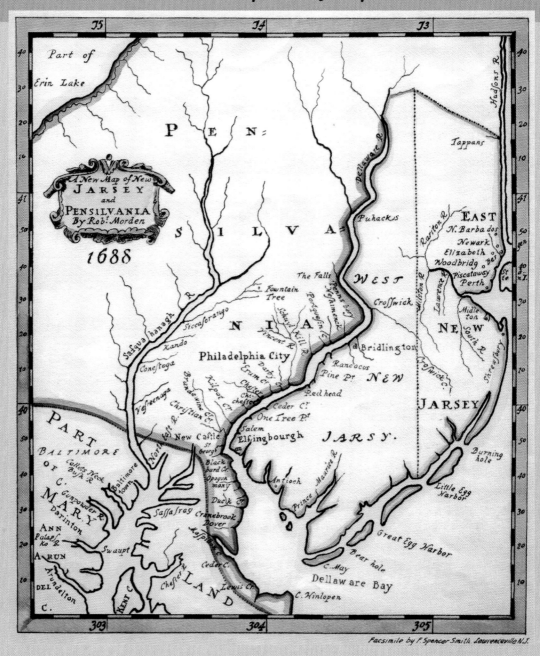

Facsimile by F. Spencer Smith. Lawrenceville N.J.

Robert Morden was a cartographer, publisher, and bookseller in London, England. Throughout his career, he drew many maps of the English colonies in North America, which were printed in various editions of his own geography books. In 1688, he published this map, entitled "A New Map of New Jarsey and Pensilvania" in his book *Geography Rectified: Or a Description of the World, the Second Edition Enlarged*. Settlements along the Delaware River are indicated and Delaware is included as part of Pennsylvania.

assembly and elected James Carteret, the illegitimate son of George Carteret, as their leader. This rebellion quickly collapsed, however, when George Carteret refused to support his son. Meanwhile, even bigger changes were on the horizon.

In 1673, the colony of New York, which still included the province of New Jersey, was reconquered by the Dutch. Since most New Jersey residents were farmers living in what was a remote rural territory, the influence of government remained minimal, and this regime change had little effect on them. Indeed, Governor Carteret and New Jersey residents continued to squabble as before.

The Dutch again surrendered New York to England in 1674. In that same year, John Berkeley, weary of the never-ending conflict between Carteret and New Jersey settlers and saddled by debt, sold his share of the province to two Quakers named Edward Byllynge and John Fenwick. Byllynge and Fenwick purchased the territory in order to establish the country's first official Quaker settlement. Byllynge became bankrupt soon after the deal was made, and his share was taken over by Quaker trustees, including William Penn, the founder of Pennsylvania.

In 1676, the province of New Jersey was divided in two by a line that extended from Little Egg Harbor on the southeastern coast to the Delaware Water Gap in the northwest corner of the territory. West New Jersey belonged to the Quakers, while East New Jersey was still owned by Carteret and dominated by Puritans. Each side established its own government and capital. In East New Jersey, the capital was Perth Amboy, while in West New Jersey, it was Burlington, which was founded in 1677. The laws of East New Jersey partook of the harsh Puritan character, including the imposition of the death penalty for thirteen specified crimes, while the

John Fenwick was born in Northumberland County at Stanton Manor, in England, in 1618. He was a lawyer who actively campaigned against the Stuart monarchy and sided with the anti-Royalist parliamentarians. He was also a Quaker who had been imprisoned for his faith. When, in 1665, Lord Berkeley put West New Jersey up for sale, Fenwick and fellow Quaker Edward Byllnge bought the territory, with Fenwick owning one-tenth of the land. His portion became modern-day Salem and Cumberland counties. After receiving the deed for the land in 1673, Fenwick prepared to emigrate to West New Jersey and encouraged other Quakers to join him, many of whom did. In 1677, Fenwick built himself a house overlooking the Delaware River in the town of Salem on a plot of land that he called Ivy Point (pictured above).

legislation of West New Jersey was based more on the Quaker spirit of forgiveness, reconciliation, and personal responsibility.

When George Carteret died in 1680, he left East New Jersey to his wife and the province's trustees. Two years later, they sold it at public auction to pay off Carteret's debts. William Penn and eleven of his associates placed the winning bid. They, in turn, divided their twelve portions of East New Jersey in half and sold them to twelve more Quakers. Together, these men were called the twenty-four proprietors, and, with their holdings in West New Jersey, they controlled most of the territory of New Jersey. The twenty-four proprietors chose fellow Quaker Robert Barclay as East New Jersey's governor.

King James II and English Authority over New Jersey

In 1685, the Duke of York, a Catholic, rose to the throne of England, becoming King James II. Two years later, he created the Dominion of New England, uniting the two Jerseys, New York, and New England under one government. He created this union for two reasons. First, England wanted to be able to draw on the colonies' manpower in the event that war broke out in North America between England and France. More important, England wanted to gain more control of its colonies, whose growing independence was worrisome. Their refusal to obey the various Navigation Acts passed throughout the seventeenth century, for example, was especially upsetting.

The Navigation Acts consisted of a series of laws that put limits on who could and could not ship cargo to England. The first two rules were simple: only English ships were allowed to transport goods from outside Europe to England, and goods from inside Europe could be shipped to England only by English ships or ships from the country that produced the goods.

Over time, these rules were expanded to include the colonies by stating that they could only export their goods to England and were not to buy goods from any country other than England. The Navigation Acts were designed to protect England's trade and boost its income. They angered the colonists, however, who resented not being able to buy, sell, and trade as they pleased. These and similar attempts by England to control the colonies and regard them primarily as a source of income would be a main cause of the colonial frustration and rage that would eventually result in the American Revolution.

The newly appointed governor of the Dominion of New England was Sir Edmund Andros. As governor of New York in the 1670s, he had tried to claim authority over East and West New Jersey. He went so far as to have Philip Carteret arrested. Courts overruled Andros, however, and the two New Jerseys continued to exist separately from New York. Even apart from this provocation, Andros was not a likable person. He was said to be loud, rude, and pompous. His insistence on obeying the Navigation Acts, along with his loyalty to the Church of England, made him quite unpopular with the colonists, especially the Quakers and the Puritans. His lack of support among the colonists would soon drive him out of power.

The Glorious Revolution

King James II's rule was also about to come to a crashing end. In 1688, the Dutch leader William III of Orange invaded Britain with his wife, Mary II, who was also James's daughter, and a large army. William marched unopposed into London to take the throne away from James. James's army deserted him. Left unprotected, he fled to France. Parliament was not sure what to do. It would be difficult to force James to return to the throne, so instead they considered his escape to be an abdication and asked William and Mary to rule as joint sovereigns. They agreed.

Without James on the throne, Andros's influence in New England disappeared completely. Knowing that he was not well liked in the colonies, he attempted to escape from Boston by

AT THE TOWN-HOUSE in
BOSTON:
April 18ʰ· 1689

SIR,

Our Selves as well as many others the Inhabitants of this Town and Places adjacent, being surprized with the Peoples sudden taking to Arms, in the first motion whereof we were wholly ignorant, are driven by the present Exigence and Necessity to acquaint your *Excellency*, that for the Quieting and Security of the People Inhabiting this Countrey from the imminent Dangers they many wayes lie open, and are exposed unto, and for your own Safety; We judge it necessary that you forthwith Surrender, and Deliver up the Government and Fortifications to be Preserved, to be Disposed according to Order and Direction from the Crown of *England*, which is suddenly expected may Arrive, Promising all Security from violence to your Self, or any other of your Gentlemen and Souldiers in Person or Estate: or else we are assured they will endeavour the taking of the Fortifications by Storm, if any opposition be made.

To Sr. Edmond Andros Knight.

William Stoughton.	*Simon Bradstreet.*	*Wait Winthrop.*
Thomas Danforth.	*John Richards.*	*Samuel Shrimpton.*
	Elisha Cook.	*William Browne.*
	Isaac Addington,	*Bartbol. Gidney.*
	John Foster.	
	Peter Sergeant.	
	David Waterhouse.	
	Adam Winthrop.	
	John Nelson.	

Boston Printed by *Samuel Green.* 1639.

Angered by the New England colonies' growing resistance to royal authority, King Charles II decided to disband the separate colonial governments and unite all of New England, New York, and New Jersey under one government. The former governor of New York and New Jersey, Edmund Andros *(above right)*, was named governor of this new Dominion of New England. Andros ruled as a tyrant, raising taxes, imprisoning innocent people, restricting freedom of the press, and demanding the individual colonies to hand over their charters. When Charles was overthrown by William and Mary, Andros was quickly seized by angry colonists. The demand for his surrender by a group of prominent Massachusetts colonists appears above left.

dressing as a woman. However, his boots peeked out from under his skirts, revealing his disguise, and he was captured. Andros was put in prison and managed to escape twice. Both times he was caught and brought back. Finally, he was returned to England, but he came back to North America in the 1690s as governor of Virginia (1692) and Maryland (1693–1694).

New Jersey in Flux

Despite this political turmoil and uncertainty, as the eighteenth century began, New Jersey was continuing to grow. Farming had increased, and crops were being sold to Europe, the West Indies, and other colonies like New York, Pennsylvania, and New England. Peter Kahn, a Swedish traveler passing through the area, wrote in his journal that in New Jersey, "every countryman had an orchard full of peach trees, which were covered with such quantities of fruit that we could scarcely walk without treading upon peaches that had fallen off," as quoted in Stein's *New Jersey*. Iron mining was developing quickly, as the area was rich in ore in the northern hills and bog iron in the south (bog iron is iron ore found in peat marshes). The timber industry was also taking off, as more and more trees were cut for lumber that was shipped to other colonies and overseas. Along the Jersey shore, sailors caught a variety of fish and harpooned whales. The whale carcasses were brought onto the land, where they were cut up for meat and for their oil, which was used in lamps.

Despite Andros's departure and William of Orange's capture of the throne, New Jersey was still not free of England's influence and control. Following Andros's fall from power, several groups lay claim to New Jersey, including descendants of the Carterets, Quakers, and the colony of New York. To clarify this chaotic situation, England's Queen Anne (daughter of James II and sister and

A View at Minisink, New-Jersey.

The former town of Minisink, New Jersey, is depicted in this eighteenth-century etching. The Minisink Valley is an area that reaches from Minisink Ford, New York, to Lackawaxen, Pennsylvania, to the Delaware Water Gap at New Jersey and Pennsylvania. It is a region of valleys that have been filled by debris from a great glacier. The area's earliest settlers were Dutch colonists wandering from the Hudson River valley toward the Delaware. In the Minisink Valley, they established copper mines and built the old Mine Road, believed to be the first 100-mile road built in America. A border war between the colonies of New Jersey and New York from 1719 to 1769 resulted in the town of Minisink becoming part of New York and eventually being renamed Port Jervis.

successor of Queen Mary) designated New Jersey a crown colony in 1702, after forcing the Quakers to surrender their charters to both halves of the territory, which from now on would be treated as a single, unified province. At the same time, Anne placed New Jersey under the rule of New York's governor. Not until 1738 would New York and New Jersey be separated for good.

Despite their unification into a royal colony, the two former halves of New Jersey continued to develop quite differently. The eastern part of the colony was primarily made up of Scottish, English, and New England settlers, while the western part was predominantly Quaker. A dwindling number of Lenape families were scattered throughout the colony. The majority of the tribe had died from measles, diphtheria, smallpox, and other diseases brought to the New World by the Europeans. Those who remained were greatly saddened by the way their homeland was being treated. While the Lenape wished to preserve the forests that had provided them with shelter and sustenance for so long, European settlers chopped them down to create more farmland or build towns. Many of the Lenape left New Jersey and moved to other colonies like New York. In another fifty years, they virtually disappeared from the region they had called home for more than 10,000 years.

CHAPTER 4

In its early days as a crown colony, the newly unified New Jersey was placed under the rule of the New York governor. Colonists protested loudly until they were given their own governor, Lewis Morris, in 1738. Despite his leadership, however, the colony still found itself struggling to define who owned precisely what land.

With a population greater than 30,000, land titles were being disputed and settlers were still refusing to pay any money to any authority for the land they occupied. Finally, the issue erupted into rioting. Hundreds of farmers remained on their properties, refusing to be evicted by either sheriffs or even the militia. Friends and family members of those arrested would often storm the jails and free them. Not knowing what else to do, the East Jersey proprietors, all Quakers, turned to King George II to ask for his help in quelling the riots and settling the question of land ownership. The petition they sent him in 1748 describes the violence and chaos of New Jersey:

Growing Anger in a Growing Colony

[G]reat numbers of men . . . entered into combination to subvert the laws and constitution of the province and to obstruct the course of legal proceedings; to which end they . . . endeavored to infuse the minds of the people that neither Your Majesty nor Your Noble Progenitors, Kings and Queens of England, had any right whatsoever to the soil or

In 1638, New Jersey finally received its own governor, independent of New York. It was hoped that the appointment of Lewis Morris *(above left)* to the position would help resolve some of the taxation and land ownership issues that were beginning to turn parts of New Jersey into a battleground. The occasionally violent disputes over titles to land continued however, as the petition *(above right)* by residents of the Burlington area to King George II indicate: "That whereas some of your Petitioners have been left unavoidably to commit disorderly riots in Defence of what they supposed their just Rights, and are now convinced that such Practices are illegal & wrong, and by no means to be persisted in, we humbly pray that this Honourable Groupe would petition his Excellency for an Act of Grace on the mildest Terms possible, and we beg it as a Favour . . . that the Titles to the Lands in Dispute may be decided by a fair Tryal before disinterested judges, that so an end may be put to the unhappy Contentions in the Country."

government of America and that Your Majesty's and their grants thereof were void and fraudulent. Having by those means associated themselves, great numbers of the poor and ignorant part of the people of the province ... broke open the jail of the county of Essex and took from thence a prisoner ... and have since that time gone on ... dispossessing some people of their estates ... plundering some people of their estates ... plundering the estates of others who do not join with them ... breaking open Your Majesty's prisons as often as any of them are committed and rescuing their accomplices from thence, and ... traveling often in armed multitudes to different parts of this province for those purposes ... Your Majesty's petitioners ... having not the least hopes or expectations that their persons or properties will be protected by their own legislatures, do find themselves under a necessity of laying this their petition at the feet of your most Sacred Majesty the gracious Guardian and Protector of all your faithful subjects.

—Text of petition provided by the New Jersey
Historical Commission

Ultimately, the question of land ownership was decided in favor of the proprietors. The settlers were either evicted or paid the proprietors for their land.

Displacement, Growth, and Simmering Anger

At the same time that many New Jersey settlers were fighting to maintain possession of their homes and land, the Lenape, the original inhabitants of that land, were also struggling to find a place to live. By the mid-1750s, the New Jersey Lenape numbered in the

A. *Der Priester welcher tauft.* TAUFE C.C. *Die Arbeiter von ihrer Nation.*
BBB *Die Tauflinge.* der Indianer D.D. *Die Indianer-Gemeine.*
in America

The Moravians were a Lutheran sect of Christianity that originated in Austria. They were deeply religious people who, like the Quakers, were committed to pacifism. The Moravians began missionary work among the Lenape in the 1740s and eventually set up thirty-two mission towns in North America. Though the missionaries hoped to "civilize" and Christianize the "heathen" Lenape, they also showed a respect for Lenape culture and spirituality that was uncharacteristic of most European settlers in the New World. In the above engraving, a Moravian minister baptizes a group of Lenape converts.

hundreds. In 1758, the New Jersey Assembly offered these few surviving members of a once thriving nation a 3,044-acre tract in Burlington County upon which to build a reservation.

The Native Americans accepted this offer and were led to their new home by the Reverend John Brainerd, a missionary to the Lenape and a trustee of the College of New Jersey (which was founded in 1746 and became Princeton University). Brainerd named the Lenape's new home Brotherton in the hopes that the Lenape and the white colonists would all live as brothers. Unfortunately, after he left the reservation in 1777, it began to fall apart. Finally, in 1796, the Oneida tribe in New Stockbridge, New York, invited the remaining Lenape to join them and spread their mats before "our fireplace, where you will eat with your grandchildren out of one dish and use one spoon," as quoted in Susan Ditmire's article "Native People of New Jersey." In 1801, the Brotherton reservation was sold, and the proceeds were given to the last of the Lenape. Brotherton was New Jersey's first and last Indian reservation (as well as America's first reservation).

Despite the many disagreements and conflicts over land and politics, the colony continued to grow rapidly. Between 1710 and 1750, the towns of Orange, Freehold, New Brunswick, Princeton, Trenton, Newton, Hackensack, Morristown, Dover, Westfield, and Plainfield were founded. By the late 1770s, the population had skyrocketed, reaching almost 80,000. Roughly nine in ten New Jersey residents were of European ancestry, mostly English, Scottish, Irish, or Scots-Irish with a scattering of Dutch, Germans, and Swedes descended from the first wave of immigration to the colony. There were also a sizable number of African Americans, nearly all of whom were slaves. Almost all of these residents were farmers, and the new towns springing up were centers of the surrounding farming communities. New Jersey had more roadways than any of the other colonies. In 1764, the first road to link Pennsylvania to New York was built, running straight through New Jersey.

New Jersey was not the only American colony to be consumed by disputes and frustrations over land, taxes, leadership, and England's intrusion into its business affairs. Indeed, all of the thirteen

THE GOVERNORS OF NEW JERSEY
BEFORE THE AMERICAN REVOLUTION

Philip Carteret	East New Jersey (1665–1682)
Edmund Andros	East and West New Jersey (1674–1681; 1688–1689)
Edward Byllynge	West New Jersey (1680–1687)
Robert Barclay	East New Jersey (1682–1690)
Daniel Cox	West New Jersey (1687–1692)
Andrew Hamilton	East and West New Jersey (1692–1698, 1699–1703)
Jeremiah Basse	East and West New Jersey (1698–1699)
Edward Hyde, Lord Cornbury	(1703–1708)
John Lovelace	(1708–1709)
Richard Ingoldesby	(1709–1710)
Robert Hunter	(1710–1720)
William Burnet	(1720–1728)
John Montgomerie	(1728–1731)
William Cosby	(1732–1736)
Lewis Morris	(1738–1746)
Jonathan Belcher	(1747–1757)
Francis Bernard	(1758–1760)
Thomas Boone	(1760–1761)
Josiah Hardy	(1761–1763)
William Franklin	(1763–1776)

The FLYING MACHINE.

This is to give NOTICE to the PUBLIC, THAT the FLYING MACHINE, kept by JOHN BARNHILL, in Elm street, near Vine-street. Philadelphia; and JOHN MASHEREW, at the Blazing star, performs the Journey from Philadelphia to New-York in two days, and from thence to Philadelphia in two days also; a circumstance greatly to the advantage of the traveller, as there is no water carriage, and consequently nothing to impede the Journey. It has already been performed to the general satisfac-

An eighteenth-century advertisement for the "Flying Machine," which performed a two-day coach ride between New York and Philadelphia, appears above. The coach rode along the King's Road, an old path that began to be turned into a road running from Philadelphia to Morrisville, Pennsylvania, in 1677. The road was extended to New York and became the main route running between Philadelphia, Trenton, and New York. The first stagecoach between Philadelphia and New York began running in 1756, a three-day, ninety-mile journey. By 1783, the "Flying Machine" had reduced the trip to two days. See the transcript on page 57.

colonies were increasingly chafing under the rule of their mother country. As England's desire to control America grew stronger, it would not be long before colonial anger would reach such a pitch that the disagreements would have to be settled on the battlefield. The distant but ominous rumblings of the approaching American Revolution were beginning to be heard.

CHAPTER 5

Despite all of the changes that New Jersey had experienced since Verrazano's first exploration of its shores 250 years earlier, the biggest developments still lay ahead. By the middle of the eighteenth century, all of the thirteen American colonies began to feel torn between allegiance to England and an increasingly urgent desire to be independent. As the years passed, it became more and more clear to the colonies that independence was absolutely necessary. One of the main sources of irritation was that England was continuing to restrict the colonies' economic freedom by enforcing the Navigation Acts and imposing taxes on some of the products the colonies used most, such as stamps and tea.

Independence, Revolution, and Statehood

The Greenwich Tea Burning

The New Jersey colonists' frustration grew until one day in the autumn of 1774, it exploded in an act of rebellion that mirrored the famous Boston Tea Party of 1773. It began in a seaport town called Greenwich, located about five miles (eight kilometers) from Delaware Bay. A British ship called the *Greyhound* had sailed up Cohansey Creek into Greenwich's harbor. The *Greyhound*'s main cargo was a huge shipment of tea from the East India Tea Company, which England had placed a tax upon. Knowing that the colonists would object to the tax and possibly try to climb on board and damage the tea, Dan Bowen, a Tory (a conservative colonist who remained loyal to England), had

As soon as the committee were chosen, they were publicly informed, that a quantity of Tea had been secretly landed at Greenwich, and that the inhabitants of that town had taken the alarm, and had chosen a *pro tempore* committee of five persons, to take care of the same until the committee of the county was chosen; the general committee then withdrew, in order to consider what should be done in the affair, and came into the following resolution, namely, That this Committee, being ignorant of the principles on which the

The tea burning that took place in Greenwich, New Jersey, on December 22, 1774, occurred just over a year after the more famous Boston Tea Party. The circumstances and actions taken, however, were remarkably similar. Like their Boston counterparts, the Greenwich colonists, angered over the taxes placed upon the tea they were forced to buy exclusively from the East India Tea Company, resolved to destroy a recently delivered shipment rather than submit to another instance of British taxation and intrusive control of colonial commerce. An account of the plot and the burning appears above in a January 9, 1775, *Pennsylvania Packet* article, above. Greenwich became one of five towns in the American colonies to "host" a "tea party." The others were Boston, Massachusetts; Charleston, South Carolina; Annapolis, Maryland; and Princeton, New Jersey.

the tea taken off the ship and stored in his cellar. His actions did not go unnoticed.

A group of Whigs (pro-independence colonists) saw what Bowen had done and gathered to make a plan. News of last year's Boston Tea Party had reached them, and they admired what those rebels had done. After several months of planning, forty of the

New Jersey colonists dressed like Native Americans and broke into Bowen's house. They took all of the tea out of the cellar, carried it to a nearby field, and set it on fire. The event went down in history as the Greenwich Tea Burning, and in 1908 a monument was erected to honor it.

The East India Tea Company was upset about its destroyed product and insisted that the people involved be arrested and punished. Company officials persuaded Governor William Franklin to take action, and he turned the job over to Sheriff Jonathan Elmer. Elmer was a Whig and supported the colonists' act of protest, so when the men came to trial, he made sure the entire jury was made up of fellow Whigs. The verdict they returned was "no cause for action," meaning no punishment was necessary.

Governor Franklin was angry with Elmer's manipulation of the judicial process, so he removed him from office and appointed none other than Daniel Bowen to head the new trial. The verdict was the same the second time around, however, and finally the East India Tea Company and Franklin gave up the fight. Many of the people who had participated in the tea burning went on to prominent political and military careers. Elmer later became one of the first United States senators from New Jersey. Franklin would turn out to be New Jersey's last royal governor.

Time for War

The Greenwich Tea Burning was a vivid example of the anger that was growing within the colonies. A large number of the colonists finally reached the point where they felt the only remaining way to protect their best interests and gain independence was all-out war with England. In New Jersey, about one-third of the population supported revolution, one-third remained loyal to England,

JEMIMA CONDICT'S DIARY AND FEARS OF WAR

Jemima Condict (1754–1779) was a young woman who lived near Morristown, New Jersey. The Condict family can be traced as far back as the late 1600s in Newark. This excerpt from Jemima's diary reveals her fears about the approaching revolution:

Monday Wich was Called Training Day I Rode with my Dear father Down to see them [the colonial militia] train there. Being Several Companys met together. I thought It Would Be a mournfull Sight to see if they had Been fighting in earnest & how soon they will be Calld forth to the field of war we Cannot tell, for by What we Can hear the Quarels are not like to be made up Without bloodshed. I have jest Now heard Say that All hopes of Conciliation Between Briten & her Colonies are at an end for Both the king and his Parliament have announced our Destruction. Fleet and armies are Preparing with utmost diligence for that Purpose. On April 23, as every Day Brings New Troubels So this Day Brings News that yesterday very early in the morning They began to fight at Boston, the regulars. We hear Shot first there: they killd 30 of our men A hundred & 50 of the Regulors.

—Diary of Jemima Condict, 1772–1779, courtesy of the
New Jersey Historical Society

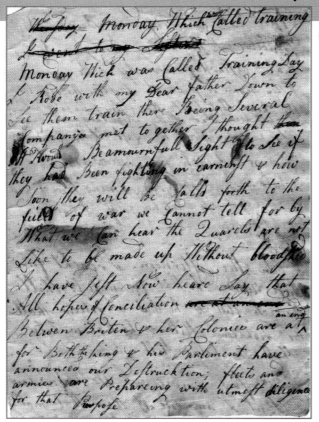

Jemima Condict was a young woman who lived near Morristown, New Jersey. She recorded the events of her life, happenings around town, the contents of sermons at her church, and reports of local births and deaths for seven years, until her early death. On October 1, 1774, Jemima made her first note concerning the growing tension between the colonies and England, commenting, "They say it is about tea." This diary entry from April 23, 1775, concerns the colonists' military preparations and news of the Battle of Lexington and Concord in Massachusetts.

and the remaining third—many of them Quaker pacifists—were neutral. Despite similar divisions of opinion in the other twelve colonies, the Continental Congress—an assembly of colonial representatives—declared independence from England on July 4, 1776, more than a year after the first armed conflict between British soldiers and colonial militia broke out in the Battle of Lexington and Concord, in Massachusetts. The American Revolution had officially begun.

New Jersey played a crucial role in the war for independence. Much of the Continental army's ammunition was made in New Jersey. General George Washington and his army spent about a quarter of the war in New Jersey, which was often referred to as the crossroads of the American Revolution because it was centrally located among the thirteen colonies and lay between the

Paulus Hook was a small island off the western shore of the Hudson River. A causeway was built between it and the mainland, making Paulus Hook a part of the main post road from New York to Philadelphia. By the 1760s, it was known for its stagecoach and ferry service to Manhattan. Paulus Hook was fortified by General George Washington at the beginning of the Revolutionary War. As depicted in the above drawing, however, the fort fell to the British in September 1776. This defeat represented the first British occupation in New Jersey. Paulus Hook remained under British control until 1783, and is now part of Jersey City.

key cities of New York, home of the British Army, and Philadelphia, home of the Continental Congress. Five major battles and 200 more minor skirmishes were fought in the state. Today, monuments and memorials to those battles and the brave men who fought them can be found throughout the state.

Industrialization

After the end of the Revolutionary War, New Jersey turned its attention to rebuilding its economy. During the 1800s, a variety of

This 1835 painting by E. I. Henry depicts the brand-new Camden & Amboy Railroad, one of the forces of industrialization that would radically transform the still largely agrarian state of New Jersey. The Camden & Amboy was the first railroad to operate in New Jersey and was one of the first steam locomotives in America. It was founded by inventor, naval architect, and transportation pioneer, John Stevens, and his sons, Robert and Edwin. In 1830, the New Jersey legislature granted a charter for the Camden & Amboy Railroad. The railroad was constructed in 1834 and passenger service began in early 1835. Its route ran between Perth Amboy, in northern New Jersey, and Camden, on the Delaware River south of Trenton and across the river from Philadelphia.

industries began to develop throughout the state, including the production of silk, iron, textiles, leather goods, soap, bricks, steel, and glass. Two major canals were built that crossed the state and carried goods between Philadelphia and New York. Railroads began to connect New Jersey with neighboring states and cities.

New Jersey's growth would again be interrupted by war in the mid-nineteenth century. It was one of the states that agreed with President Lincoln's decision to end slavery. Although no battles

Though densely populated and home to many heavy industries, New Jersey remains an important and productive agricultural state. Cranberries, like the packaged ones at right, are one of its most important and popular crops. The Lenape were the first to harvest the cranberries in the southern and central portions of the state. Cranberry cultivation in New Jersey probably began in the 1840s. Today, there are about 3,500 acres of cranberry vines under cultivation. New Jersey is the third-largest producer of cranberries, behind Massachusetts and Wisconsin. It produces about 10 percent of the nation's cranberries.

were fought on its soil, New Jersey sent thousands of its citizens to fight in the Civil War on the side of the Union. After the war was over, New Jersey took up where it left off and continued to prosper. Two large companies got their starts in New Jersey in the mid-1800s: Welch's Grape Juice Company and Campbell's Soup.

In the years immediately following the Civil War, 30 percent of New Jersey's residents were living in cities, a remarkable shift away from the state's traditionally agricultural life. Many of these city residents were recent immigrants from Ireland and Germany who were employed in the state's growing industrial and manufacturing sector. The manufacturing of oil, steel, chemicals, rubber, and clothing supported a booming economy and an exploding population. By the 1920s, there were more than 3.1 million people living in New Jersey, fifteen times the number of state residents at the beginning of the nineteenth century. Much of this increase was due to immigration from Europe, especially from Germany, Italy, Ireland, Poland, and Russia. New Jersey still maintained its rural heritage, however, especially in the central and southern areas of the state, where dairy and poultry farms appeared.

In 1917, the United States entered World War I (1914–1918). New Jersey contributed to the war effort by producing the battleships and ammunition used by the Allies overseas. Like most other states throughout the country, New Jersey was hit hard by the Great Depression of the 1920s and 1930s, and many of its once-thriving factories were forced to close. The onset of American involvement in World War II in the early 1940s bolstered the flagging economy, and once again New Jersey found itself producing the ammunition, battleships, and communication equipment needed in the war. The city of Paterson produced more airplane engines than any other city in the world, and hundreds of thousands of the state's citizens served in battle.

New Jersey Today

In the second half of the twentieth century, many residents of New Jersey left their small and crowded city apartments for brand-new houses in suburban communities that were suddenly appearing on former farm fields throughout the state. At the same time, manufacturing began to slump and factories closed. These two developments resulted in the deterioration of many New Jersey cities. Buildings were abandoned, and many of the people left behind became mired in poverty. In the 1980s, a concentrated effort was made to improve New Jersey's cities. Urban renewal lured both business and residents back to some cities. These public efforts, coupled with a new wave of immigration to urban New Jersey by people from Latin America, Asia, and Africa, have injected the state's cities with new vitality and optimism.

Today, more than 8.5 million people live in New Jersey, the most densely populated state in the Union. This population pressure has resulted in the development of much of the state's open land. Indeed, when traveling through the central and northern portions of the state, it is often hard to imagine how New Jersey could ever have gained its nickname, the Garden State. State authorities must always balance the need to provide a place for all these people to live with the imperative to protect New Jersey's rural heritage and natural beauty.

Though New Jersey would be unrecognizable to the Lenape today, New Jersey remains what it had been to the Lenape and the earliest European settlers—a peaceful, vibrant, tolerant, and bounteous place to live. For the 8 million New Jerseyans who live there today, it is simply the special place they call home.

1524 —— Giovanni da Verrazano is the first European explorer to land on what will become New Jersey.

1609 —— Henry Hudson sails along the New Jersey coast up the river that separates New Jersey from New York and now bears his name.

1614 —— Dutch explorer Cornelius Mey sails into the mouth of the Delaware River and builds a small fort near the present-day town of Gloucester.

1630s —— Swedes and Dutch move into the part of New Netherland that will become known as New Jersey.

1655 —— Peter Stuyvesant, director general of New Netherland, forces most of the Swedes out of the region.

1660 —— The Dutch set up the territory's first permanent village, called Bergen (part of present-day Jersey City).

1664 —— England takes control of New Netherland and gives part of it to Lord John Berkeley and Sir George Carteret, who rename the territory New Jersey.

1674 —— Berkeley sells his share of the land to Edward Byllynge and John Fenwick.

1676 —— New Jersey is divided into two separate sections—East and West New Jersey.

1682 —— William Penn and other Quaker proprietors buy East New Jersey.

1688 —— The Glorious Revolution removes King James II from the throne.

1702 —— East and West New Jersey are reunited by England, and New Jersey becomes a royal colony ruled by the governor of New York.

1738 —— New Jersey receives its own royal governor and becomes independent of New York.

1746 —— The College of New Jersey is founded. It will become Princeton University.

1748 —— Land riots break out as proprietors try to establish their ownership of the land.

1758 —— The colony's remaining Lenni Lenape are offered a tract of land in Burlington County to create a reservation called Brotherton.

1766 —— Rutgers University is founded as Queen's College.

1774 —— Unhappy colonists conduct the Greenwich Tea Burning to protest British taxes.

1776 —— New Jersey, along with the twelve other American colonies, declares its independence from England. It becomes one of the thirteen original states in the United States of America.

December 25–26, 1776 — General George Washington crosses the Delaware River and surprises Hessian troops at Trenton, New Jersey, seizing much-needed supplies and artillery.

January 3, 1777 — General Washington and the Continental Army attack the British in Princeton, New Jersey, and force them to flee. Following the battles at Trenton and Princeton, Washington had driven the British from most of New Jersey.

1783 —— Princeton briefly serves as the nation's capital (as it also will in 1799).

1784 —— Trenton briefly serves as the nation's capital.

1787 —— New Jersey is the third state to ratify the U.S. Constitution.

PRIMARY SOURCE TRANSCRIPTIONS

Page 9: Translation of an excerpt of a July 8, 1524, report to King Francis I written by the explorer Giovanni da Verrazano concerning his experiences and discoveries in the New World

Transcription
...After the tempest suffered in the northern parts, Most Serene King, I have not written to Your Majesty that which was experienced by the four ships which thou hadst sent by the Ocean to discover new lands, thinking that thou hadst been certified of everything— how we were compelled by the impetuous force of the winds to return to Brittany with only the distressed *Normanda* and *Dauphine*; where having made repairs, Your Majesty will have learned the voyage we made with them, armed for war, along the coasts of Spain; later, the new disposition with the *Dauphine* alone to continue the first navigation; having returned from which, I will tell Your Majesty what we have found ...

Page 23: Excerpt of an indenture signed by James, Duke of York, on June 23, 1664, granting the territory that would become New Jersey to George Carteret and John Berkeley

Transcription
This indenture made the three and twentieth day of June, in the sixteenth year of the reign of our sovereign Lord, Charles the Second, by the grace of God of England, Scotland, France and Ireland, King Defender of the Faith, &c., Annoq. Domini, 1664. Between His Royal Highness, James Duke of York, and Albany, Earl of Ulster, Lord High Admiral of England, and Ireland, Constable of Dover Castle, Lord Warden of the Cinque ports, and Governor of Portsmouth, of the one part: John Lord Berkeley, Baron of Stratton, and one of His Majesty's most Honourable Privy Council, and Sir George Carteret of Saltrum, in the County of Devon, Knight and one of His Majesty's most Honourable

Privy Council of the other part: Witnesseth that the said James Duke of York for and in consideration of the sum of [ten?] shillings of lawful money of England to him in hand paid before the sealing and delivery hereof by the said John Lord Berkley and Sir George Carteret, the receipt whereof the said James Duke of York, doth hereby acknowledge, and thereof doth acquit and discharge the said John Lord Berkley and Sir George Carteret forever by these presents hath granted, bargained, sold, released and confirmed, and by these presents doth grant, bargain, sell, release and confirm unto the said John Lord Berkley and Sir George Carteret, their heirs and assigns for ever, all that tract of land adjacent to New England, and lying and being to the westward of Long Island, and Manhitas Island and bounded on the east part by the main sea, and part by Hudson's river, and hath upon the west Delaware bay or river, and extendeth southward to the main ocean as far as Cape May at the mouth of the Delaware bay; and to the northward as far as the northermost branch of the said bay or river of Delaware, which is forty-one degrees and forty minutes of latitude, and crosseth over thence in a strait line to Hudson's river in forty-one degrees of latitude; which said tract of land is hereafter to be called by the name or names of New Caeserea or New Jersey . . .

Page 31: An April 18, 1689 demand for the surrender of Sir Edmund Andros

Transcription
At the Town-house in Boston:
April 18th 1689

Sir,
Our selves as well as many others the inhabitants of this town and places adjacent, being surprised with the people's sudden taking to arms, in the first motion whereof we were wholly ignorant, are driven by the present exigence and difficulty to acquaint your Excellency, that for the quieting and security of the people inhabiting this countrey from the imminent dangers they many ways lie open,

and are exposed unto, and for your own safety; we judge it necessary that you forthwith surrender, and deliver up the government and fortifications to be preserved, to be disposed according to order and direction from the Crown of England, which is suddenly expected may arrive, promising all security from violence to your self, or any other of your gentlemen and soldiers in person or estate: or else we are assured they will endeavour the taking of the fortifications by storm, if any opposition be made.

To Sr. Edmond Andross Knight.
[Signed]

Page 41: A circa 1780 advertisement for the "Flying Machine" stage coach between New York and Philadelphia

Transcription
The Flying Machine.
This is to give notice to the public, that the Flying Machine, kept by John Barnhill, in Elm Street, near Vine Street, Philadelphia; and John Masherew, at the Blazing Star, perform the journey from Philadelphia to New-York in two days, and from thence to Philadelphia in two days also; a circumstance greatly to the advantage of the traveler, as there is no water carriage, and consequently nothing to impede the journey. It has already been performed to the general satisfaction of many genteel people. They set off from Philadelphia and New York on Mondays and Thursdays, punctually at sunrise, and change their passengers at Prince Town, and return to Philadelphia and New York the following days: passengers paying ten shillings to Princeton, and ten shillings to Powle's Hook opposite to New York, ferriage free, and three-pence each mile any difference between. Gentlemen and ladies who are pleased to favour us with their custom may depend on due attendance and civil usage, by their humble servants, John Barnhill and John Masherew.

GLOSSARY

abdication Giving up power or authority officially.

allegiance Faithful devotion to one's country, a person, or a cause; loyalty.

carcasses Dead bodies.

deferred Put off until a future time; postponed.

dispute An argument or disagreement.

edible Capable of being eaten; safe to eat.

enterprising Able to take over a complicated or difficult project.

enticement Something that attracts or lures in; bait.

gristmill A mill for grinding grain.

lured Attracted or drawn in.

militia A group of citizens who receive military training but who are on call only for emergencies.

persecute To cause constant suffering to, often because of political or religious beliefs.

pompous Characterized by excessive self-esteem or exaggerated dignity.

proprietor One who has a title to something; an owner.

sovereign The chief estate in a monarchy, such as a king or queen.

tanneries Places where animal hides are converted into leather.

Tory A colonist who remained loyal to England and supported continued English rule of the colonies.

trinkets Small ornaments like glass beads or cheap jewelry.

trustees A group of people or a firm that is legally responsible for another person's property.

Whig A colonist who supported independence from England.

FOR MORE INFORMATION

The Lenni Lenape Historical Society
Red 2
Fish Hatchery Road
Allentown, PA 18103
Web site: http://www.lenape.org

New Jersey Chamber of Commerce
50 West State Street
Trenton, NJ 08608

New Jersey Historical Society
52 Park Place
Newark, NJ 07012
(973) 596-8500
Web site: http://www.jerseyhistory.org

New Jersey Reference Services
New Jersey State Library
CN 520
Trenton, NJ 08625

Web Sites

Due to the changing nature of Internet links, the Rosen Publishing Group, Inc., has developed an online list of Web sites related to the subject of this book. This site is updated regularly. Please use this link to access the list:

http://www.rosenlinks.com/pstc/neje

FOR FURTHER READING

Fredeen, Charles. *New Jersey*. Minneapolis, MN: Lerner Publications, 2001.

Knight, James E. *The Village: Life in Colonial Times*. Mahwah, NJ: Troll Communications, 1998.

Marsh, Carole. *New Jersey Indians!* Peachtree City, GA: Gallopade International, 2004.

Moran, Mark, and Mark Sceurman. *Weird N.J.: Your Travel Guide to New Jersey's Local Legends and Best Kept Secrets.* New York, NY: Barnes & Noble, 2003.

Stein, R. Conrad, and Matthew Kachur. *New Jersey.* Danbury, CT: Children's Press, 1998.

Sterngrass, Jon. *New Jersey: Life in the Thirteen Colonies*. Danbury, CT: Children's Press, 2004.

Stewart, Mark. *New Jersey Native Peoples*. Chicago, IL: Heinemann Library, 2003.

Stewart, Mark. *Uniquely New Jersey*. Chicago, IL: Heinemann Library, 2003.

Streissguth, Thomas. *New Jersey: The Thirteen Colonies*. San Diego, CA: Lucent Books, 2001.

Weatherly, Myra S. *The New Jersey Colony.* Chanhassen, MN: Child's World, 2003.

BIBLIOGRAPHY

Armstrong, Harry. *New Jersey Firsts: The Famous, Infamous, and Quirky of the Garden State*. Philadelphia, PA: Camino Books, 1999.

Ditmire, Susan. "Native People of New Jersey." The American Local History Network. Retrieved October 2004 (http://www.usgennet.org/nj/state/Lenape.htm).

Elson, Henry William. "New Jersey," in *History of the United States of America*. New York, NY: MacMillan Company, 1904. Retrieved September 2004 (http://www.usahistory.info/colonies/New-Jersey.html).

Green, Howard L. "A Synopsis of New Jersey History." Official State of New Jersey Web site. July 1996. Retrieved September 2004 (http://www.state.nj.us/hangout/synopsis.htm).

Lurie, Maxine N., and Marc Mappen. *The Encyclopedia of New Jersey*. New Brunswick, NJ: Rutgers University Press, 2004.

Moragne, Wendy. *New Jersey*. New York, NY: Benchmark Books, 2000.

New Jersey City University. "History of New Jersey." 2001. Retrieved September 2004 (http://faculty.njcu.edu/ckarnoutsos/Chronology.htm).

Pomfret, John E. *Colonial New Jersey*. New York, NY: Charles Scribner's and Sons, 1973.

State of New Jersey. "A Short History of New Jersey." Undated. Retrieved September 2004 (http://www.state.nj.us/hangout_nj/assignment_history_ll.html).

Wick, Steve. "*Half Moon* Arriving." Newsday.com. Retrieved October 2004 (http://www.newsday.com/community/guide/lihistory/ny-historyhs214a,0,5846973.story?coll=ny-lihistory-navigation).

Wroth, Lawrence C., ed. *The Voyages of Giovanni da Verrazano*. Translated by Susan Tarrow. New Haven, CT: Yale University Press, 1970.

PRIMARY SOURCE IMAGE LIST

Page 5 (bottom): A color aquatint entitled *Passaic Falls in New Jersey, 1798,* by Alexander Robertson.

Page 7: An untitled, circa 1640 drawing of a Lenape couple by Peter Lindestrom.

Page 9 (left): A July 8, 1524, report to King Francis I written by the explorer Giovanni da Verrazano concerning his experiences and discoveries in the New World. Housed in the New-York Historical Society.

Page 13 (bottom right): A lithograph by George Haywards of a circa 1648 map of New Netherland made by Adriaen van der Donck. Housed in the New-York Historical Society.

Page 16 (top): An untitled seventeenth-century print by Thomas Campanius Holm depicting trading activity between Swedish settlers and Lenape. It first appeared in a book published in Stockholm, Sweden, by J. H. Werner in 1702, entitled *Kort beskrifning om provincien Nya Swerige uti America, som nu för tiden af the Engelske kallas Pensylvania* (A short description of the province of New Sweden, now called, by the English, Pennsylvania, in America). Housed in the Historical Society of Pennsylvania.

Page 20: A late seventeenth-century portrait of Sir George Carteret. Housed in the Special Collections and University Archives, Rutgers University Libraries, New Brunswick, New Jersey.

Page 23: An indenture signed by James, Duke of York, on June 16, 1664, granting the territory that would become New Jersey to George Carteret and John Berkeley.

Page 24: A late seventeenth-century painting entitled *The Quaker Meeting,* by Egbert van Heemskerk. Housed in the Library of the Religious Society of Friends, London, England.

Page 26: A 1688 map by Robert Morden entitled "A New Map of New Jarsey and Pensilvania," published in his book *Geography Rectified: Or a Description of the World, the Second Edition Enlarged.*

Page 28: An eighteenth-century painting of Ivy Point, the home of John Fenwick, built in 1677. Housed in the Salem County Historical Society, Salem, New Jersey.

Page 31 (left): An April 18, 1689, demand for the surrender of Sir Edmund Andros, signed by William Stroughton, Simon Bradstreet, and Wait Winthrop, among others. Printed in Boston, Massachusetts, in 1689 by Samuel Green.

Page 31 (right): A seventeenth-century oil painting of Sir Edmund Andros by Mary Beale. Housed in the Virginia Historical Society.

Page 33: An eighteenth-century etching entitled *A View at Minisink, New-Jersey.* Housed in the Rare Book and Special Collections Division of the Library of Congress, Washington, D.C.

Page 36 (top): A circa 1750 oil portrait of Lewis Morris by John Wollaston. Housed in the National Portrait Gallery, Smithsonian Institution, Washington, D.C.

Page 36 (bottom): A circa 1748 petition to King George II from residents of Burlington, New Jersey, requesting a fair settlement of land ownership issues in the northern parts of the colony.

Page 38: An engraving that depicts a Moravian minister baptizing Lenapes. The engraving appears in a 1757 German-language booklet entitled *Kurze, zuverlaszige nachricht von der unter dem namen der Bomisch-Mahrischen bruder bekannten kirche Unitas Fratrum herkommen, lehr-begriff, aussern und innern Kirchen-Verfassung und gebrauchen* (A short, reliable report from the church of the Unitas Fratrum, known under the name of the Bohemian-Moravian Brethren, concerning canon, external and internal church constitution and customs). A copy of the booklet is housed in the Reeves Library at Moravian College, Bethlehem, Pennsylvania.

Page 41: A circa 1780 advertisement for the "Flying Machine" stagecoach between New York and Philadelphia, placed by John Barnhill and John Masherew.

Page 43: A January 9, 1775, *Pennsylvania Packet* newspaper article on the Greenwich, New Jersey, tea burning that occurred on December 22, 1774.

Page 46: An April 23, 1775, entry from the diary of Jemima Condict. Housed in the New Jersey Historical Society.

Page 48: An 1835 painting by E. I. Henry entitled *Camden and Amboy Railroad.* Housed in the Special Collections and University Archives, Rutgers University Libraries, New Brunswick, New Jersey.

Page 49: An early twentieth-century package label for Jersey Belle Brand New Jersey Cranberries. Housed in the Ocean Spray Cranberries, Inc. Corporate Archives, Lakeville-Middleboro, Massachusetts.

INDEX

About the Author

Tamra Orr is a full-time writer living in the Pacific Northwest. She has authored more than thirty nonfiction books for children and families, as well as countless magazine articles, many of them concerning American history. She has a particular interest in the histories of the thirteen original colonies.

Photo Credits

Cover © Delaware Art Museum, Wilmington, USA, Howard Pyle Collection/ Bridgeman Art Library; pp. 1, 26, 46 from the Collections of the New Jersey Historical Society, Newark, New Jersey; pp. 5 (top), 9 (right), 13 (top) © Bettmann/Corbis; p. 5 (bottom) I.N. Phelps Stokes Collection, Miriam and Ira D. Wallach Division of Art, Prints and Photographs, The New York Public Library, Astor, Lenox and Tilden Foundations; p. 7 © Hulton/Archive/Getty Images; pp. 9 (left) 77365d, 13 (bottom) 73823, 16 (bottom) 73871t, Collection of The New-York Historical Society; p. 16 (top), The Historical Society of Pennsylvania, (Am 1702 Cam); pp. 20, 48 Special Collections and University Archives, Rutgers University Libraries; pp. 23, 36 (bottom) New Jersey State Archives, Department of State; p. 24 reproduced with permission of the Religious Society of Friends in Britain; p. 28 Salem County Historical Society, Salem, New Jersey; p. 31 (left) Courtesy Massachusetts Archives, Massachusetts Archives v. 242: p. 365; p. 31 (right) Virginia Historical Society, Richmond, Virginia; p. 33 Library of Congress Rare Book and Special Collections Division; p. 36 (top) National Portrait Gallery, Smithsonian Institution/Art Resource, NY; p. 41 The Library Company of Philadelphia; p. 43 The Warren Lummis Library of the Cumberland County Historical Society, Greenwich, New Jersey; p. 47 courtesy of Richard LaRovere; p. 49 the Ocean Spray Cranberries, Inc., Corporate Archives.

Photo Researcher: Sherri Liberman